FAMILY CELEBRATIONS

FAMILY CELEBRATIONS

Prayers, Poems, and Toasts
for Every Occasion

JUNE COTNER

**Andrews McMeel
Publishing**

Kansas City

02 03 RDC 10 9 8 7

Library of Congress Cataloging-in-Publication Data
Family Celebrations: prayers, poems, and toasts for every occasion / [compiled by] June Cotner.
    p.   cm.
  Includes index
  ISBN 0-8362-7856-9 (hardcover)
  1. Family—Religious life. 2. Prayers. 3. Religious poetry, American. I. Cotner, June, 1950–   .
  BV4526.2.F325 1999
  082—dc21   98-48036
                                            CIP

Design by Holly Camerlinck
Typeset by Coleridge Design and Imaging
Illustrations by Tanya Maiboroda

www.junecotner.com

————— ATTENTION: SCHOOLS, CHURCHES, AND BUSINESSES —————

Andrews McMeel books are available at quantity discounts with bulk purchase for educational, business, or sales promotional use. For information, please write to: Special Sales Department, Andrews McMeel Publishing, 4520 Main Street, Kansas City, Missouri 64111.

FOR JIM, KYLE, AND KIRSTEN
TOGETHER FOR ALWAYS—

we walk
holding hands
our fingers
woven together
hanging between us
like a basket
soft but strong
and snugly knit
with room enough
for love to fit

RALPH FLETCHER
(EXCERPTED FROM *ROOM ENOUGH FOR LOVE*)

CONTENTS

13   ❧ HOLIDAYS ❧

A Letter to Readers

I have always loved family celebrations! This book grew out of that love. About twenty years ago, I started a file box of poems and clippings divided into various categories such as weddings, anniversaries, and memorial services. It was my desire to gather original selections to bring to our family celebrations. I recently started searching for a book containing selections that could be read aloud at family gatherings, hoping to add great readings to my collection. After an extensive search, I could find no such book. *Family Celebrations: Prayers, Poems, and Toasts for Every Occasion* was born!

When I think of family celebrations, I think of the specialness of families and how important it is to honor and celebrate the events that touch our lives. Family celebrations connect us to one another and link memories between us, extending our ties through many generations. They underscore our recognition of the importance of the milestones of our lives, and the lives of our loved ones. Family gatherings help us share important rites of passage, such as weddings and new babies. They also help us to draw near one another and the Divine, such as when we celebrate a loved one's life during a memorial service.

In this book, you will find what you need for celebrating and blessing life's grand events as well as selections for sanctifying the more ordinary transitions such as a new job, moving day, or retirement.

Here are a few tips for using the selections in *Family Celebrations*:

- If you are attending an event where you might be called upon to give a toast, memorize a short selection such as "The Best Man's Toast" on page 29 . Don't be caught yelping, "Here's to the bride and groom!"

- Some selections, such as "Blessing of the Athletes" on page 183 and "A Blessing for Family" on page 91, are particularly good for reading in unison.

- Many of the selections can be read by children ten years and older. Perhaps about thirty minutes before serving dinner, you could open the book to the chapter on graces and ask a child to select one to be read aloud. Children love to be included! If children aren't present, offer the honor to a senior relative.

- On occasions when you can't be together for a celebration, copy a favorite passage onto a blank greeting card and send it to your loved one. Please be sure to credit the poet and this book.

My editor, publisher, and I believe there will be future interest for a second volume of *Family Celebrations*. Please send any submissions that would fit the format of this book to the address below. If you'd like to submit for a category not represented in this book, I welcome those submissions too. Keep in mind that all submissions *must* be universal, not your personal ode to Dad.

Another book for which I am now accepting submissions is *Family Traditions: A Treasury of Inspiring Ideas for Connecting and Nurturing Families*. If you have a favorite family tradition, I'd love to hear from you! My vision is that *Family Traditions* will be the same size as *Family Celebrations*, a nice, easy-to-hold, gift book. Please limit your essays describing your favorite family tradition to no more than two hundred words, so each selection will fit on one page. Typed submissions are always appreciated (with your name, address, and phone number at the top of each page). If you include a self-addressed stamped envelope, you'll eventually hear from me.

I'm always open to compiling collections that help nurture and support families. If you have an idea for a book that would help enrich family life, I'd love to hear from you!

June Cotner
P. O. Box 2765
Poulsbo, WA 98370

T H A N K S

This book would not have come about without the support of a loving family; a terrific agent and friend, Denise Marcil; a talented and caring editor, Patty Rice; the backing of an enthusiastic publisher, Andrews McMeel Publishing; and wonderful selections received from countless contributors.

I feel especially blessed by the joys of my family: my husband, Jim Graves; my daughter, Kirsten Cotner Myrvang; my son, Kyle Myrvang; and many dear relatives in my extended family—who all give me many reasons to celebrate.

In all, more than four thousand submissions were considered for *Family Celebrations*. That's on top of favorite selections I've collected for many years, culled from more than one thousand books.

Beginning with my first anthology, *Graces*, I used a test-market group to evaluate the selections in each of my anthologies to help determine the final content for each book. I believe this process has helped create books that appeal to people of all faiths and beliefs and that are accessible to general readers.

Specifically, I would like to thank each member of my test-market group: Father Paul Keenan (author of *Good News for Bad Days: Living a Soulful Life* and cohost of the national ABC radio program, *Religion on the Line*), Rabbi Rami M. Shapiro (storyteller, poet, and author of *Minyan: Ten Principles for Living a Life of Integrity* and four other books), and Reverend Gary W. Huffman (coauthor of *The Bible: A to Z* and pastor of First Presbyterian Church, PCUSA, Shelbyville, Indiana).

My editor, Patty Rice, and her editorial assistant, Jennifer Fox, graciously gave of their time to critique a very lengthy test-market manuscript. Joyce Standish, an independent editor with her own company ("papers" in Las Vegas, Nevada) provided her usual support and astute recommendations.

Deepest appreciation goes to my husband, Jim Graves; my daughter, Kirsten Cotner Myrvang; my son, Kyle Myrvang; and my cousin and her husband, Margie Cotner Potts and Jim Potts, for providing such valuable feedback on the manuscript. As always, I'm indebted to many dear friends who carved time into their busy schedules over a two-week period to evaluate the manuscript and make sure the selections were appropriate for the book: Lynn Eathorne Bradley, Deborah Ham, Patricia L. Huckell, and Susan C. Peterson.

My life is so blessed by my acquaintance with over five

hundred regular contributing poets to my anthologies. I'm grateful for their enthusiasm, patience, and understanding that sometimes it can take months before I can respond to their submissions.

Five of my contributing poets graciously offered their time to provide a professional critique and evaluation of *Family Celebrations*. Specifically, I would like to thank Susan J. Erickson (a talented, "late bloomer" poet who started writing at age fifty-five and was published in *Bless the Day*), Maureen Tolman Flannery (author of *Secret of the Rising Up: Poems of Mexico*), Margaret Anne Huffman (award-winning journalist, author of *Through the Valley: Prayers for Violent Times* and twenty-nine other books), Arlene Gay Levine (author of *39 Ways to Open Your Heart*), and Barbara Younger (author of *Purple Mountain Majesties: The Story of Katharine Lee Bates and "America the Beautiful"*). Special thanks to Katherine Younger for giving me a fifteen-year-old's perspective on the selections.

Pulling double duty critiquing the manuscript were my two employees Cheryl Edmonson and Alena Ellen Fisse-Karr. In particular, I'd like to thank Cheryl for her good cheer, her organizational skills in handling huge stacks of paperwork, and her eagerness in assuming responsibility for a great deal of the "business" end of creating anthologies (such as securing permissions), which frees up my time for reading and promotion. Also, I'd like to thank Courtney

Froemming for her terrific publicity work in promoting my books, Monique Denhart and Lacey Menne for assisting with word processing, Shawna Erickson for proofreading, Kevin Jennings for making my computer more obedient, and Roger Block, for general all-around support.

The following individuals at Andrews McMeel Publishing have been enthusiastic and extremely supportive in promoting my books: Hugh Andrews, national sales director/book division, Jay Hyde, director of marketing, and Shannon Guder, publicist.

In addition to being very labor-intensive, creating anthologies is an expensive endeavor. I'm especially grateful to publishers and license holders who recognize this and either waive or reduce their permission fees so that all of us can benefit from the words of grace and wisdom contained in *Family Celebrations* as well as other anthologies.

My last and most sincere appreciation goes to the Divine One, who guides me on my journey of creating spiritual poetry anthologies, reminding me of the sacred in the ordinary, the sublime in the divine, and the mystery that brings all of us together.

FAMILY CELEBRATIONS

GENERAL TOASTS

TOAST TO A GOOD LIFE

(from *The Merry Wives of Windsor*)

Heaven give you many, many merry days!

WILLIAM SHAKESPEARE
(1564–1616)

General
Toasts

GRATITUDE

To our
Friends who have become Family
and our
Family who have become Friends—
May you be blessed with the same
love and care you've given us.

MARY MAUDE DANIELS

*General
Toasts*

~ 3 ~

MAY YOU HAVE WARM WORDS

May you have warm words
on a cold evening,
A full moon on a dark night,
And the road downhill all the way
to your door.

AUTHOR UNKNOWN

*General
Toasts*

TOAST TO THE NOW

I heard someone say:
Yesterday is history
tomorrow is a mystery
today is a gift
and this is why
this moment is called the Present.

Listen, look, taste, touch,
breathe. The Present.

SUSAN J. ERICKSON

EACH DAY

Each day the first day:
Each day a life.

DAG HAMMARSKJÖLD
(1905–1961)

THANKS!

For all that has been—Thanks!
For all that shall be—Yes!

DAG HAMMARSKJÖLD
(1905–1961)

General
Toasts

⌒ 7 ⌒

As If

Dance as if no one were watching,
Sing as if no one were listening,
And live every day as if it were your last.

AUTHOR UNKNOWN

TOAST TO DAUGHTERS

To every daughter
to yours
to mine
from the youngest
to the oldest.
A wish for happiness
for a lively spirit
the will to be herself
a desire to help others
laughter on every horizon
peaceful dreams
and a loving life.

JOAN STEPHEN

REMEMBRANCE

Let today embrace the past with remembrance
and the future with longing.

KAHLIL GIBRAN
(1883–1931)

*General
Toasts*

A Thousand Days

A thousand days
like today!

AUTHOR UNKNOWN

*General
Toasts*

GRACES

A MORNING GRACE

I accept this new day as your gift,
and I enter it now with eagerness;
I open my senses to perceive you;
I lend my energies to things of goodness and joy.
Amen.

RITA SNOWDEN

Graces

MORNING PRAYER

God of Light,
Spirit of Compassion,

You open up
the morning skies
again before us.
You breathe in us
the breath of life.

Be our guide
in this new day.
Be present with
and in us.

Graces

Heal us.
Lift us.
Stir us.
Gift us.

Let us be a blessing
and a reflection of You.

Amen.

DEBORAH COOPER

Graces

A Child's Noontime Grace

Thank You, God, for food to eat—
For milk and bread, for sandwich meat.
Thank You, Lord, for tasty cheese.
But do I *have* to eat these peas?

JEAN CONDER SOULE

Graces

A Native American Grace

O Morning Star! when you look down upon us, give us peace and refreshing sleep. Great Spirit! bless our children, friends, and visitors through a happy life. May our trails lie straight and level before us. Let us live to be old. We are all your children and ask these things with good hearts.

THE INDIANS OF THE GREAT PLAINS:
NATIVE AMERICA, TRADITIONAL

GRACE OF COMPASSION

Lord
This day
At this table
In this company
Touch us in this place.
Fill our hearts with Your love,
Keep our sympathy and compassion
Always fresh and
Our faces turned towards heaven
Lest we become hard, and forget,
As we love You, we shall gift
Each other with patience
And Love.

PATRICK E. LOUKES

Graces

GRACE BEFORE SLEEP

How can our minds and bodies be
Grateful enough that we have spent
Here in this generous room, we three,
This evening of content?
Each one of us has walked through storm
And fled the wolves along the road;
But here the hearth is wide and warm,
And for this shelter and this light
Accept, O Lord, our thanks to-night.

SARA TEASDALE
(1884–1933)

Graces

A BUDDHIST GRACE

(In Buddhist monasteries before every meal,
a monk or a nun recites these Five Contemplations.)

This food is the gift of the whole universe—
the earth, the sky, and much hard work. May we
live in a way that is worthy of this food. May we
transform our unskillful states of mind, especially
that of greed. May we eat only foods that nourish
us and prevent illness. May we accept this food
for the realization of the way of understanding
and love.

AUTHOR UNKNOWN

Graces

BLESS OUR MEAL

May God bless
our meal and grant us a
compassionate and understanding heart
toward one another.

MOUNT ST. MARY'S ABBEY,
WRENTHAM, MASSACHUSETTS

Graces

A Grace for a Gathering

Bless our family with peace and joy,
let our words to each other be kind,
and our actions gentle.
May the love that we share be *Your* love,
so that each of us can always say:
Lord, it is good for us to be here!

ANNE VOGEL

A Grace for Friends

Traveler . . . be at peace
You are welcome here
Our door is open.
Hands extend across the table
Bread is broken in shared contentment
Hearts are warmed and healed anew.
Let this house
Be a harbor in breeze or gale
Traveler . . . fair winds be at your sail.

STEPHEN KOPEL

Graces

WEDDINGS

A Wedding Toast

May your love be firm,
and may your dream of life together
be a river between two shores—
by day bathed in sunlight, and by night
illuminated from within. May the heron
carry news of you to the heavens, and the
    salmon bring
the sea's blue grace. May your twin thoughts
    spiral upward
like leafy vines, like fiddle strings in the wind,
and be as noble as the Douglas fir.
May you never find yourselves back to back
without love pulling you around
into each other's arms.

James Bertolino

What Greater Thing

(From *Adam Bede*)

What greater thing is there for two human
    souls,
than to feel that they are joined for life—
to strengthen each other in all labor,
to rest on each other in all sorrow,
to minister to each other in all pain,
to be one with each other
in silent unspeakable memories . . .

GEORGE ELIOT
(1819–1880)

WEDDING TOAST

grow always
grow together
find your music
and dance

GAAR SCOTT

A Friend's Wedding Toast

Here's to this fine couple.
May their joys be as bright as the morning,
and their sorrows but shadows that fade
in the sunlight of love.

AUTHOR UNKNOWN

THE BEST MAN'S TOAST

When the roaring flames of your love
have burned down to embers,
may you find that you've married your best
friend.

AUTHOR UNKNOWN

In One Another's Souls

The moment I heard my first love story
    I began seeking you,
not realizing the search was useless.
Lovers don't meet somewhere
    along the way.
They're in one another's souls
    from the beginning.

RUMI
(1207–1273)

Adapted by Eleanor Munro
from the translation by A. J. Arberry

WEDDING TOAST:
A MARRIAGE FOR ALL SEASONS

May your love be as invigorating as the air of
autumn,
As persevering as the winter's cold,
As refreshing as the return of spring,
And as gratifying as the fullness of summer.
May your marriage be blessed abundantly on
your wedding day
And continue to grow through all the seasons of
your love.

JAN DUNLAP

THEY KNOW

That it's more than the eager early
plans whispered in the slim glow
of the hammock moon. More than
the persistent hunger of desire,
the soft curve of muscle,
the convincing charm of chemistry.

That it's about keeping your balance.
Maneuvering around corners, edges,
angles, the invisible borders of moods.
Steering clear of the sheer cliffs
of history, the tyranny of genes,
the seduction of power. That without honor,
love can be short as the life of a dancer.

That these promises are more
than an ancient arrangement of language.
They bring forth light and a new vision.
They know that what they create here
must be soft and steady
as the breathing of birds,
strong and sure as the
weathered wings of an angel.

ALLISON J. NICHOL

The Riddle of Three Words

When you think
you have found
the right person
to say them to

you must make sure
you mean them
with all your life
and have earned
the right to say them.

You must also wonder
if the other will
believe and accept them.

Mere volume will not
convince either of you.

If you hear them
said to you
you must wonder
if they are truly meant,
if you are indeed
the one for whom
they are intended,
if you deserve them,
and exactly what they mean.

If these conditions
are all satisfied
and you can say
and receive them
in all faith

they will seem
the most beautiful
short poem
in any language

and you will pray
you may say
and hear it
every day
the rest
of your life.

NORBERT KRAPF

Second Marriage

We came late together, O God of second chances, making the discovery of our love even sweeter. We honor all that has brought us to this moment, trusting in your promise to make all things new. Give us many years to share so that we can weave them together with vibrant strands of loyalty, kindness, and warmth into a coverlet of married love, a wedding gift from You.

MARGARET ANNE HUFFMAN

Weddings

Overheard at a Cowboy's Wedding

As you begin your wedded life
joined together as husband and wife,
Pull together as a matched team,
neither going to the extreme.
Lasso kindness and hold her tight,
never let love out of your sight.

Now hitched for a lifetime project,
for one another show respect.
Saddle up for the blissful ride,
corral some humor on the side. (You'll need it!)

Don your hats and pull on your boots,
Parson pronounced you in cahoots.
As you walk towards the western skies,
at all costs, avoid the cow pies.

JUDY A. BARNES

SOUL MATES

The quiet miracle
Of a man and woman
Uniting as one,
To travel the road of happy destiny
Together,
Is like a sacred haven in the sky,
The feeling of having arrived
Without ever leaving.

JENNIFER M. SPENCER

Weddings

A DAUGHTER'S WEDDING DAY TRIBUTE

Dearest Parents: On our wedding day, as my husband and I take our vows and make promises to each other, I make this promise to you as well. Even as I take him into my heart and life, I promise to keep you, parents dear, in my heart and life always.

On this day, know that our love is not divided; it is multiplied, and you are embraced with the full measure of love and promises that he and I share here today.

For I know that I am able to love and cherish him so much because you loved and cherished me first.

SHARON OSTRANDER REED

A Parent's Wedding Toast

When children find true love,
parents find true joy.
Here's to you two,
may your joy and ours last forever.

AUTHOR UNKNOWN

I Love You

I love you for what you are, but I love you
yet more for what you are going to be.
I love you not so much for your realities
as for your ideals.
I pray for your desires that they may be great,
rather than for your satisfactions,
which may be so hazardously little.
You are going forward toward something great.
I am on the way with you,
and therefore I love you.

CARL SANDBURG
(1878–1967)

ANNIVERSARIES

FOR OUR ANNIVERSARY

This much I know is true—
the secret to lasting love
is in the details—
a hand to hold
when I'm feeling sad,
the circle of your arms
around me
when the cold night air closes in.
I can tell you anything
and you won't laugh
or run away.
Partners for life you and I,
we're marathoners
who've learned to keep the pace
straight and steady.
When I say the word "us"
I think of the day we met
and all the days in between,
that sense of place, of belonging
that begins and ends with you.

MARY EASTHAM

MILESTONE ANNIVERSARY

The couple we honor today speaks a language that's made a lifetime of commitment possible. It is a thousand "I told you so's" swallowed in patience; a hundred "if you had's" silently forgiven, and dozens of daily "I love you's" never forgotten or taken lightly.

We who can only eavesdrop around the edges of this ongoing conversation, hear between its lines a cherishing where these lovers, who are friends, laugh together at the end of rough days, cry together when needed, and awaken after all these years turned toward the other with still more to say. They delight in new things yet to discover, surprises still to learn about their love for one another, new interests and directions to share— all leading to even more reasons they're glad to be married.

Continue to bless and inspire the writers of this rare one-of-a-kind tale.

MARGARET ANNE HUFFMAN

TWO HEARTS

Two hearts
comforting, reaching,
holding each other
through the ups and downs of
everyday existence

Two people
nurturing and raising children together
through tears, fears,
laughter, and smiles

Two individuals
working hard to make the world
a better place
for their children and grandchildren

Two hearts
dancing together,
waltzing to the heartbeat of
love's eternal tunes

Two partners
whose loving is the simplicity of spring
yet able to withstand stormy weather
Your love keeps shining
brighter
and embraces those around you

Happy Anniversary!

SHERRI WAAS SHUNFENTHAL

Anniversaries

An Anniversary Toast

Let the purpose of all marriages
and friendships alike
be the deepening of the spirit
and the enrichment of the soul.

AUTHOR UNKNOWN

Anniversaries

~ *48* ~

GOLDEN WEDDING ANNIVERSARY

We close our hands
over that moment
brief as years,
that never-passing remembrance

when time
stopped for us
and space

with a sweep
tuned our quivering strings
firm

and music without words
said
Right for each other

and we were.

IDA FASEL

GOING FOR THE GOLD

Five decades together
come good or come bad
One half a century
Some joyous, some sad
Fifty years of living
puts hearts to the test
Fifty years of loving
has brought out your best!

ARLENE GAY LEVINE

Anniversaries

≺ *50* ≻

THE BEST IS YET TO BE

Grow old along with me!
The best is yet to be,
The last of life, for which the first was made:
Our times are in his hand . . .

ROBERT BROWNING
(1812–1889)

Anniversaries

YOU WERE BORN TOGETHER

(from *The Prophet*)

You were born together, and together you shall
  be forevermore.
You shall be together when the white wings of
  death scatter your days.
Aye, you shall be together even in the silent
  memory of God.
But let there be spaces in your togetherness,
And let the winds of the heavens dance
  between you.
Love one another but make not a bond of love:
Let it rather be a moving sea between the shores
  of your souls.
Fill each other's cup but drink not from one cup.
Give one another of your bread but eat not from
  the same loaf.
Sing and dance together and be joyous, but let
  each one of you be alone,
Even as the strings of the lute are alone though
  they quiver with the same music.

Give your hearts, but not into each other's
    keeping.
For only the hands of Life can contain your
    hearts.
And stand together, yet not too near together:
For the pillars of the temple stand apart,
And the oak tree and the cypress grow not in
    each other's shadow.

KAHLIL GIBRAN
(1883–1931)

Anniversaries

NEW BABIES

BABY FAIR

Baby fair,
Baby sweet;
Angel kisses
On your feet.

Tiny dancer
On the wing;
Your new voice
Is here to sing.

Baby love,
Baby mild;
Welcome, welcome,
Brand-new child.

LINDA ROBERTSON

*New
Babies*

New Baby

This place is radiant
with the simple, perfect grace
of you, beginning.

Tended by heartbeats,
you are the seed
of a tangle of dreams,
jewel tones, opening
like wildflowers
in spontaneous brilliance,

visions of recipes
and heirlooms handed down.
Already we dance
at the celebrations
your life will bring,

*New
Babies*

where we will find ourselves
called together again
and again, reminded,
warmed,
as this braid of lifelines
that makes us family
grows more and more entwined.

KATE SIMPSON

*New
Babies*

Prayer for a New Baby

We are grateful
for this new being
who is small in body
but great in Soul,
who has come
into our midst
as a gift.
May we be sensitive
to the Sacred
as we nurture
and learn from
this child.
Give us patience.
Give us strength.
And grant us
wisdom and love
to help this child
learn to sing
his own song.

*New
Babies*

ANNE SPRING

A PARENT'S PRAYER

We call unto the Source of Life
in thanksgiving for the wonder of this gift of life.
We are humbled by the blessings
and responsibilities of parenthood
and our participation in the miracle of creation.

May we learn to love without smothering.
May we learn to house without imprisoning.
May we learn to give without imposing.
May we learn to live today,
that yesterday and tomorrow
might find their own way in the world.

We give thanks to Life for the gift of life,
and stand in wonder
before the awesome task of parenting that lies
    before us.
Blessed is the Way of Life that makes parent
    rejoice with child.

RABBI RAMI M. SHAPIRO

*New
Babies*

ADVICE TO MY
NIECE AT HER BIRTH

You will explore, hand over hand,
this world, pushing the limits
far beyond wall, house, yard.
You will jump feet first
into puddles, delighting in
the splash; a rainbow of
droplets clinging to your hair.

Remember this courage, exploration,
blind faith that your feet will hold you.
Wrap it up like a smooth
pebble from the shore,
enclose it as a precious keepsake.

There are those who will tell you
Be Cautious, Don't Trust, Stay Safe,
who would make you
doubt the strength you feel
in your own legs.

I tell you
the world is dangerous
for those who see danger while
enclosing themselves in iron cages.
The world is sorrow for those
who cling to tears.

Unwrap your pebble, child,
hold it tight and take the plunge,
jump feet first into joy.

NITA PENFOLD

*New
Babies*

FROM THIS DAY FORTH

May our arms give you rest.
May our arms give you comfort.
May they always give you a shoulder to cry on.

From this day forth, our dearest one,
our lives and hearts are intertwined.
You are our child, a gift from God,
our treasure sublime.

ELIZABETH CAMPBELL

CHRISTENINGS

THE STARMAKER

This child
in this world
searches for the Starmaker.
Your life will be filled with dance and prayers,
magic, and laughter.
You will reach for the heavens,
and each star will shine brightly just for you.
Your life will mirror the one who leads you,
and the path that is scattered with stardust
will always be a safe one.
From those who love you will come
the motivation to shine, to be genuine and
    faithful.
Behind your smile will linger their influence.
A tender touch will guide you every day,
and grace will illuminate your soul.
Love will be good to you and
the world will be yours.

Christenings

That is a promise.
The Starmaker will give everything to
this child
in this world
one star at a time.

LORI EBERHARDY

Christenings

A CHRISTENING PRAYER

O God of all creation,
You breathe life into every living thing,
Your Spirit hovers near us
Protecting us, holding us, warming us
As a parent holds a child.

Come now and embrace this family
With your eternal love
And bless their child that he/she
May grow in grace and dignity
And find joy at every turn.

Sustain this family as they nurture their child,
As they learn together, laugh together,
And share in the mystery of life together.
In unity may they excel in love and forgiveness,
Valuing most highly the simple joy of being
    together.

Amen.

KIM V. ENGELMANN

CHRISTENING

Christen
this child,
Dear Lord,
with all your
grace and healing,
your love and protection.
Bring this child
into your
light,
forever and ever.
Amen.
Thank you.

PAULA TIMPSON

BABY BLESSING

(Note: Insert baby's name on all lines.
For a baby boy, substitute appropriate pronouns.)

O Holy One, we gather here with joy on the occasion of the christening of _____. Your gentle hands have cradled this child to life and have gifted the earth with a unique expression of your love. Give to those who will care for this child strength, courage, and wisdom as they begin this journey of responsibility.

Bless _____ that she may grow strong in body and spirit. May her lips speak the truth, may her heart find love, and may her feet always walk in the way of peace. May her special gifts be recognized and developed that she may know the joy of sharing them with others.

May your Spirit watch over and protect _____ both now and in the days to come.

_____, may the power and love of the Holy One bless you now and be with you always.

MOLLY SRODE

A Christening
Celebration Grace

Holy God, Creator of all life,
Bless _____, whom we have sprinkled
Today with the water of faith and love.
Thank you for all new life, for each new day,
And for food and family and friends. Amen.

BARBARA YOUNGER

PRAYER OF BLESSINGS

May you be blessed with a spirit of gentleness,
a heart that is tender.

May you be blessed with a spirit of strength,
shining within you.

May you be blessed with a spirit of compassion,
a fervent caring.

May you be blessed with a spirit of courage,
daring to be who you are.

May you be blessed with a spirit of openness,
understanding, and respect.

May the earth hold you.
May the wind lift you ever up.
May the fire draw and warm you.
May the water quench and soothe your soul.
Amen.

DEBORAH COOPER

BIRTHDAYS

THE FORTY POEM

Think of forty nights
and days, forty riddles
that amaze, forty thieves of love.

Imagine forty tons of squash,
forty daffodils of purple, forty hillsides
expressing clover.

Wake to forty doves cooing
to the morning, forty minnows that leap
the sun, forty ducks who've dreamed

Of platypuses. Taste forty green
grapes, forty blue. Sip the juice
of forty plum-shaped stones.

JAMES BERTOLINO

Birthdays

A Birthday Toast

We wish you joy on your birthday
And all the whole year through,
For all the best that life can hold
Is none too good for you.

AUTHOR UNKNOWN

Birthdays

~ 73 ~

A Child's Birthday Grace

Dear God,

Before I make a wish
And blow out the candles
I'll take a moment
To admire my cake and
To look at the faces
Around me.
Thank you for family,
And thank you for friends,
Thank you for cakes
With plenty of frosting,
And for one more candle
Every year.

Amen.

BARBARA YOUNGER

A BIRTHDAY WISH

I do not wish you joy without a sorrow,
Nor endless day without the healing dark,
Nor brilliant sun without the restful shadow,
Nor tides that never turn you against your bark.
I wish you love, and strength, and faith, and wisdom,
Goods, gold enough to help some needy one.
I wish you songs, but also blessed silence,
And God's sweet peace when every day is done.

DOROTHY NELL MCDONALD

Birthdays

GRADUATIONS

DESTINY

You may be moved in a direction
You do not understand,
Away from the safe, the familiar,
Towards a vision that is blurry,
Yet still pounds against
The doors of your dreams,
Screams for recognition,
Petitions for understanding,
Whispers for acceptance.
Out towards distant possibilities,
You are propelled by a fire,
You will never fully comprehend,
But cannot extinguish.

SUSAN NORTON

As You Set Off

Let each place
      where you stand
tell what it knows of you.
Let differences draw you.
Let the soil
      whisper
to your feet
      as you pass.
Let the want of a place to rest
  elevate you to that level—
    without a bed
    without a home
    without a country,
      kin to all.
Let the kindness of strangers
    feed your hunger.
  Disburse   your   kindness
    as though it were
      bread
      and
      fish.

Let the shady places beckon you
　　to lie down
　　　　　　in the cool grass
　　　and be calmed
when there is unrest in you.
Let the countries question you.
Let the questions
　　　　　　flow over you
like mountain rain
　　　and wash
　　the dust of the road
　　from your feet.

MAUREEN TOLMAN FLANNERY

A WISH FOR THE GRADUATE

I cannot help but smile
as I remember a shy five-year-old,
lunch box in hand, waiting for the bus
on the first day of school.
And now, here we are.
You, beaming in your cap and gown,
poised on the brink of adulthood.
Me, basking in your happiness.
Commencement is a true milestone,
not an ending, but the beginning
of a new phase in your life.
To say "I'm proud of you" seems inadequate,
but know that I *am* proud.
I only hope you will someday recognize
the significance of all you've accomplished.
My wish for you is a future
filled with love, hope, and success.
The knowledge you've gained
is the key that will open the door
to many bright tomorrows.

Graduations

AMY MALLETT

PHILOSOPHY

Be a seeker of visions—
And a hunter of dreams.
Be alert and excited
And proud of your life.
Dance with all music
And sing with all songs.
Be awestruck with wonder
And inspired by nature.
Shun what is wrong;
Show wisdom and class.
Honor each promise;
Love friend and foe.
Laugh with the happy
And cry with the sad—
Live for tomorrow—
But save yesterday.
Run with the wind
And savor the moment.

JOAN STEPHEN

From Mom,
On Graduation Day

It is with pride and joy—and a touch of sadness—that I watch you graduate from high school. Time has betrayed me—that moment when I first held you, time seemed eternal—yet it has rushed us to this milestone day—too fast, too fast.

You will always remember this first step into adulthood; I will always remember your very first step!

You are thinking of your cap and gown; I am thinking of the name tag dangling around your neck in kindergarten.

You are receiving graduation gifts; I am receiving dandelion bouquets.

You are hearing "Pomp and Circumstance";
I am hearing "Little Red Caboose."

You see me as I am; I see you as you are—
and as you were.

Today, your vision is fixed on the future; for a
moment, I am glancing back. You are counting
your achievements; I am counting my blessings—

It is with pride and joy—and a touch of
sadness—that I watch you graduate from high
school!

BETTI J. MARVEL

I F—

If you can keep your head when all about you
    Are losing theirs and blaming it on you,
If you can trust yourself when all men doubt you,
    But make allowance for their doubting too;
If you can wait and not be tired by waiting,
    Or being lied about, don't deal in lies,
Or being hated, don't give way to hating,
    And yet don't look too good, nor talk too wise:

If you can dream—and not make dreams your
    master;
If you can think—and not make thoughts
  your aim;
If you can meet with Triumph and Disaster
    And treat those two impostors just the same;
If you can bear to hear the truth you've spoken
    Twisted by knaves to make a trap for fools,
Or watch the things you gave your life to, broken,
    And stoop and build 'em up with wornout
      tools:

If you can make one heap of all your winnings
    And risk it on one turn of pitch-and-toss,
And lose, and start again at your beginnings
    And never breathe a word about your loss;
If you can force your heart and nerve and sinew
    To serve your turn long after they are gone,
And so hold on when there is nothing in you
    Except the Will which says to them: "Hold on!"

If you can talk with crowds and keep your
    virtue,
Or walk with Kings—nor lose the common
 touch,
If neither foes nor loving friends can hurt you,
    If all men count with you, but none too
    much;
If you can fill the unforgiving minute
    With sixty seconds' worth of distance run,
Yours is the Earth and everything that's in it,
    And—which is more—you'll be a Man, my
    son!

RUDYARD KIPLING
(1865–1936)

FAMILY REUNIONS

FAMILY RE-UNION

We come together

one yet many;
each from
a different path
to an intersection
of time and memory.
We travel under
the same sky
brilliant with stars,
sleep beneath
the changing moon.
We will leave
not as strangers,
but as pilgrims
on this rich earth.

ANNE SPRING

*Family
Reunions*

ROOTS

Like a tall tree
Resilient and strong,
We stand rooted . . .
In family traditions.
We stand rooted . . .
In family love.
We stand committed . . .
To our children
And our children's children.
We uphold every branch—
The lineage increases
And our roots . . .
Grow exceedingly deep.

Like the tallest oak
surviving many ages,
We stand rooted . . .
In our noble distinction.
We stand rooted . . .

Family
Reunions

In family pride.
We cling to the roots . . .
Which bind us by blood
And through it all . . .
Our family stands.

ALICE FAYE DUNCAN

Family
Reunions

THIS GATHERING
OF GENERATIONS

May we, this gathering of generations,
forge forward to the future
and culminate the dreams of our ancestors.

May we, this gathering of generations,
preserve our collective past
as we share and cherish our stories.

Let this blessed occasion
remind us
that when a family embraces
its common bonds,
it becomes more than
scattered individuals with a connection.

May we, this gathering of generations,
create and celebrate
our heritage, our strength, our unity.

JAYNE ENGLAND BYRNE

*Family
Reunions*

A Blessing for Family

May our family be blessed with comforts of the physical
        And riches of the spirit.
May our paths be lit with sunshine
        And sorrow ne'er darken our doors.
May our harvest be bountiful
        And our hearth ever welcoming.
May we celebrate together in times of joy
        And comfort one another in times of sorrow.
And mostly:
May we always stay together
        And share the laughter, the love, and the tears
           As only family can.

DANIELLE BRIGANTE

*Family
Reunions*

APPRECIATING
SIBLINGS

For There Is No Friend Like a Sister

For there is no friend like a sister
In calm or stormy weather;
To cheer one on the tedious way,
To fetch one if one goes astray,
To lift one if one totters down,
To strengthen whilst one stands.

CHRISTINA ROSSETTI
(1830–1894)

*Appreciating
Siblings*

SISTERS

Safeguard our secrets
Salvage our mistakes
Scratch our itches
Scatter our seriousness
Stash our pranks
Soften our heartaches
Season our lives

MARIAN OLSON

Appreciating
Siblings

WHAT MAKES YOU AWARE

Little sister, you are young—
that's the secret of your seeing.
The luxury of simply being
opens up the way for love.

I've seen you give something you prize
without a thought for recompense.
I've seen you say a sacred Yes
to people, places, things, to life.

The green fields speak without words
of what you are and what makes you aware
of the drop in your center, the essence of prayer.
As you take your place in the grown-up world

don't try to be like me too soon.
I'd do well to be like you.

KATHY CONDE

*Appreciating
Siblings*

ALWAYS

Ever there for me
in quiet ways

My brother, my friend
for all our days

ARLENE GAY LEVINE

*Appreciating
Siblings*

A CELEBRATION

I want to celebrate you.
I am truly blessed to be a part of your world.
I learn from you, I admire you, I love you.
You are my own personal star that follows me
    around
and shines down on me.
You light my life with magic and wonder.
Such a gift of love.
You are a part of my soul.
You own a piece of my heart.
Your loving spirit provides a constant parade
of emotions that warm my heart.
I feel complete knowing you are near.
I feel empty without you.
I want to celebrate you,
yesterday, today, and tomorrow.

LORI EBERHARDY

Appreciating
Siblings

HOUSEWARMINGS

HOME SWEET HOME

For the comfort you'll find
And the dreams you will sleep.
To the dinners you'll prepare
And the company you'll keep.

To all the new joys
You'll share while you're here
We wish you great happiness,
Good tidings, and cheer.

DAWN M. MUELLER

Housewarmings

A TOAST FOR YOUR NEW HOME

May life's good fortune
And blessings, too
Live here in this house
For as long as you do.

DARLENE A. CROCE

HOUSE BLESSING

(Ask those in the room or vicinity to form a
circle and hold hands. A candle and perhaps some
other meaningful symbols —flowers, stones, a
brick, a blanket, a loaf of baked bread, a child's
toy, sacred text, etcetera—may be placed in the
center of the circle on a table.)

For all that you have provided to bring us to
this day, Loving Spirit, we give you thanks. We
acknowledge the gifts of hands which labored,
hearts which dreamed, and minds which planned in
order that this place of home might come into being.

Make of this space a sanctuary, a place of haven
for our bodies and souls. Bless these walls with
laughter and joy and the company of loved ones.
Strengthen this roof to embrace anger and
disappointment. Support this foundation in order to
cradle the deepest of sorrows and bear every hurt.

Spirit of Compassion, inspire those who will
live here to extend hospitality to strangers and
welcome to friends. Continue to make us into a
family, so that we may transform this stone and
wood into a home. Amen.

MELISSA J. GRAHAM

Housewarmings

FOR A NEW HOUSE

Tonight we come together
to make this house our own,
to celebrate that certainty
amid so much unknown.

We thank the ones who built it
of brick and wood and pane,
the walls to grant us safety,
the roof against the rain.

But we know it isn't finished,
and we accept our part:
filling it with meaning,
building it by heart.

This house won't be a paradise:
We'll fight. We'll feel alone.
But then we'll come together,
and this house will be our home.

Housewarmings

The joys and sorrows yet to come,
the worst winds that have blown:
We'll love each other here,
and this house will be our home.

TIM MYERS

Housewarmings

A HOUSEWARMING TOAST

May your windows shine through sun and snow
and your lawns grow
smooth and green without a weed

May each room fulfill its promise
of everything you dreamed and bring serenity
when you desire it

May those who love you feel welcomed
and refreshed, and all the others sense
the loving spirit of this space

May your home be a place of energy and peace

MARIAN OLSON

Housewarmings

HOME

(excerpt)

> It takes a heap o' livin' in a house
> t' make it a home . . .

EDGAR A. GUEST
(1881–1959)

Housewarmings

A House Blessing

Bless this house,
O Lord, we pray.
Let Your joy
shine here today.
Fill each corner
with Your grace.
Make this home
a peaceful place.
Let laughter ring
throughout the halls.
Bring harmony
to these four walls.
May all who enter
be at rest
as Your love touches
each and every guest.

NANCY LYNCH WEISS

Housewarmings

Housewarming Toast

Bless this new home for it is a sacred place.
May its walls protect those who live within,
yet open wide to any who seek hope and
    sanctuary,
for this is a house where compassion
and acceptance are renewable natural resources.
Let this be a house where miracles
are an act of faith, a way of life.
Let this be a house that strengthens
the fabric of goodwill in the world.

SUSAN J. ERICKSON

Housewarmings

MEMORIAL SERVICES

HOPE

In this time of sorrow
Help us to remember and know
Deeply,
That if we simply turn to You
Our hearts will be comforted
Our loads will be lightened
Our souls will be understood.
Amen

JENNIFER M. SPENCER

WINTER COMES

always too soon,
before our hearts are ready
to let go.

Let us hold closely,
through the dark and cold,
the memory of summer,
and the promise.

Let the memory
and the promise
shine within us.

Good-bye comes
always too soon,
before our hearts are ready
to let go.

*Memorial
Services*

Let us hold closely,
through the dark and cold,
the memory of her (his) presence,
and the promise.

Let the memory
and the promise
shine within us.

DEBORAH COOPER

*Memorial
Services*

TO THE FOUR WINDS

Your children
   grandchildren
   great-grandchildren
   gather

The gone-befores
   are here with us
   in our memory
   in our keeping

We hold fast
   to all you taught us
   what we learned
   from your living

We give you back now
   to the earth
   to the sky
   wind and water

We bury sorrow
　　sing you outward
　　fly with you
　　hearts open

You are the seedpod
　　in its bursting
　　replenishing
　　the earth

MAUDE MEEHAN

Memorial
Services

MEMORIAL PRAYER

Source of Life,
Spirit of Compassion,
we give thanks,
from the fullness of our hearts,
for the life that we remember
in this gathering.
Let the meaning of her (his) life
live on in us.
May the light that she (he) has given us
shine on in our own lives
and hearts and memories.
Help us to find the courage
and the faith
we need each day
to carry on.
Open a way of hope before us.
Mend our hearts and teach us
to be comforters
of one another.

DEBORAH COOPER

SPEAKING TO ANGELS

(on the loss of an unborn child)

How near you were to us.
Gently embracing our lives
For such a short time.
Weaving a living thread
That suddenly paused,
Then leaped eternity.
In the stilled caress of your treasured memory,
We will speak to angels.

ANNIE DOUGHERTY

*Memorial
Services*

MEMORIAL SERVICE

This present day.
This absent one.
We are gathered
to remember
————,
gone from view,
not from heart.
Grant a safe passage
from this earth
of wild beauty
to places unknown.
Give to those
who are left—
time to mourn,
time to heal,
and time to reflect
on the memory
of the love we shared.

ANNE SPRING

A Memorial for a Pet

Dear God, Creator of all creatures great and small,

We have lost our beloved pet, and we gather today with sadness in our hearts. Yet we are here to celebrate the life of _____. We remember the playful moments, the quiet moments, and the love we shared. These are the memories of our friend that we will treasure always. (You may ask each person to share a memory of the pet.) We thank you for the days we spent with _____, for pets everywhere, and for all of the wonderful creatures that you have placed upon our earth. Amen.

BARBARA YOUNGER

Memorial
Services

A Shared Bond

Although we must continue,
and leave them far behind,
we are never beyond their embrace—
they live on in the mind.
As we gather strength once more
to do what we must do,
the bond of shared lives will remain,
untouchable and true.

JANET LOMBARD

NORTHWEST INDIAN
MEMORIAL ON DEATH

Do not stand at my grave and weep.
I am not there.
I do not sleep.
I am a thousand winds that blow.
I am the diamond glint on snow.
I am the sunlight on ripened grain.
I am the autumn rain.
When you awake in the morning hush,
I am the swift uplifting rush
Of birds circling in flight.
I am the stars that shine at night.
Do not stand at my grave and weep.
I am not there.
I do not sleep.

AUTHOR UNKNOWN

*Memorial
Services*

HOLIDAYS

Valentine's Day Toast

May our love always be as courageous
and forgiving as a child taking its first steps.
May our love open wide like the petals
of the magnolia revealing its perfect imperfection.
May our love be as wild as the dance
of fireflies, as joyful as Handel's
Hallelujah Chorus, as playful as river otters,
as satisfying as a bowl of soup on a cold day.
Yes, all these things and more, more, more.

SUSAN J. ERICKSON

St. Patrick's Day

May the Irish hills caress you.
May her lakes and rivers bless you.
May the luck of the Irish enfold you.
May the blessings of St. Patrick behold you.

AUTHOR UNKNOWN

ON PASSOVER, WE REMEMBER

Around this table
we celebrate the
Survival, Perseverance,
And Faith
Of those wandering spirits
Who escaped from their shackles,
Emerging towards freedom
To bring forth a
Nation from which
We grow, and for our
Future generations
To continue in
Freedom and Peace,
To always draw
Strength from those who
Went before.

PAULA E. KIRMAN

Holidays

LIBERATION

On Passover we speak liberation:
the freeing of the body to go its own way;
the freeing of the mind to think its own thoughts;
the freeing of the heart to feel its own fires;
the freeing of the soul to find its own place.

On Passover we speak of love:
the loving of the body and the coming to our
    senses;
the loving of the mind and the coming to sense;
the loving of the heart and the coming to
    Meeting;
the loving of the soul and the coming to
    Meaning.

May the spirit of Passover inspire us to liberate
    our world for love.
Amen.

RABBI RAMI M. SHAPIRO

THE BLOOMING OF EASTER

Easter is blooming with color—
A bouquet of every known shade.
The pink blended hues of a sunrise;
Mixed in with some orange marmalade.
The soothing blue tones of a river—
Reflections from bright, sunny skies.
The purple and yellow of blossoms
Attracting the gold butterflies.
The cardinals are showing off crimson
As they dart between leaves of new green
Making the blooming of Easter
Like nothing the world has foreseen.

JOAN STEPHEN

Holidays

EASTER

Dear God, today we celebrate the triumph of light over dark, day over night, truth over lie. We'll take this message with us into the uncertainties of tomorrow, hearing Your promise in the songs of birds who begin singing again before the storm has fully ended. They know all along that clouds cover, not banish, the sun.

MARGARET ANNE HUFFMAN

EARTH DAY
(April 22)

O God of whirling galaxies, rain forests and rivers, tides and thunderstorms, we've been too busy to notice how our choices affect our world. At last we're paying attention: You gave us a gift but we were careless and now it's broken. We gather today, repentant, hopeful, and determined to restore, cleanse, and bring new life to earth, wind, and creature. Let us share Your imagination; let us be Your fingers as we tend this gift, which holds and carries us all.

REV. LYNN JAMES

In Celebration of the Family

(for Family Week, the week
that ends with Mother's Day)

Join and bless this family, O God, so that its circle be where quarrels are made up; where errors are forgiven and solutions found. Family is where we first find love, acceptance, security; where we are first celebrated and cherished. Keep our home fires burning; You, O God, are the fuel from which we gain warmth, safety, and inspiration.

MARGARET ANNE HUFFMAN

Holidays

A Mother's Day Toast

Please lift your glasses high to honor mothers,
Everyone's first love,
Who risk their lives giving birth,
Who respect the heart-thoughts of their children,
Who know "mother" is not the same as "smother."

To mothers,
Who always believe we can and will improve,
Who love us deeply enough to let us go,
Who end every phone call with "I love you,"
Who never give up hoping for our happiness.

We thank them for their strength,
We honor them for their suffering,
We forgive them their mistakes,
For in becoming aware of their limitations,
We learn to acknowledge our own.
To our mothers—and their love.

SUZANNE C. COLE

If (for Mothers)

(with thanks to Rudyard Kipling)

If you can keep your head when all your children
Are bumping theirs and crying out for you;
If you can calm yourself when they all wrangle,
Yet make allowances for their wrangling too;
If you can bathe and dress your children,
Then see them play in the dust or rain,
And hear them cry, "He tore my ribbon!"
Then sigh, and clean them up again . . .

If you can read a child a story
While bread is baking for next day,
And keep an eye on supper cooking,
Yet watch the other kids at play;
If you can sleep with an eye open
To listen for a wail or woe,
And rise to chase away an ogre
Or rub a back, or other comfort show;

If you can bear to have the truth you've spoken
Scorned by adolescents who only heed their peers;
Or watch the child you've nurtured growing willful
And pray he'll straighten up in later years;
If you have dreams for all your children
But have to change those year by year;
If you can give each one your blessing
And send them forth with words of cheer;

If you can talk with children and not grow
      childish;
If you can work hard, yet have time to play;
If when your children hurt you, you forgive them
And start afresh with each new day;
If you have filled each living minute
With love and care (almost divine),
You'll have an honored place in heaven—
And what's more . . . you'll be a Mom like mine!

DORIS LAND MUELLER

Mother, You Inspire Me

Mother, you taught me,
To be steward of the talents God gave me
With appreciation for both abilities and
    limitations.
You reminded me that we all remain unfinished,
And need to continue to learn and grow.
You said to stand up for what I believe in,
Remember that I can never be perfect
But am accountable for choices made,
Be not seduced by the glitz and glitter
Of the superficial and insincere,
They bring but brief and shallow pleasures.
And, finally, lead a life that matters,
One that contributes to another's betterment,
Along with my own.
Today, I want you to know that as powerful
As your teachings were, the highest inspiration
Came from simply watching you live.

SUSAN NORTON

FOR MEMORIAL DAY

(from the *Gettysburg Address*)

The world will little note, nor long remember, what we say here, but it can never forget what they did here. It is for us the living, rather, to be dedicated here to the unfinished work which they who fought here have thus far so nobly advanced. It is rather for us to be here dedicated to the great task remaining before us—that from these honored dead we take increased devotion to that cause for which they gave the last full measure of devotion—that we here highly resolve that these dead shall not have died in vain. . . .

ABRAHAM LINCOLN
(1809–1865)

Holidays

~ *133* ~

The Finest Tribute
(for Memorial Day)

The sleeping princes of this world are mourned today.
We say good night to them over again
with our wreaths and our tears.
No one knows as well as the family
of one of these soldiers the meaning of Memorial Day.
We see the crosses row on row, exclaim over the poppies;
but the boy gone from our lives
makes us realize the meaning of it all:
The lady we call the Statue of Liberty
holds out her glowing torch to all races and creeds,
proclaiming the blessedness of freedom.
Today we stand at the grave of the Unknown Soldier again,
and in our hearts comes a strange feeling, wordless.
Is there a wreath large enough to match the beauty
of his devotion to his country? Only one.
It is in the faces of the children marching in the parade—
carrying the flag.

Holidays

He loved the red, white, and blue enough to die for it.
He wants no wreath except this—
the flag he chose as his eternal flower—
Freedom blooming forever.

MARION SCHOEBERLEIN

Holidays

In Memoriam

Each mother said a silent prayer—
This wreath's for you, my son.
They say they do not know your name;
But I know you're the one.
The one I held when you were small;
The one I rocked for hours—
The one who tramped across far hills
To bring home leaves and flowers.
The one I taught to read a book—
The one who ran so fast;
The one who walked to school with friends
On days that are now past.
They say they do not know your name;
But I know you're the one—
The one who fought the bravest fight—
This wreath's for you, my son.

JOAN STEPHEN

A Father's Day Toast

To Dad,
May the love and respect we express toward you
make up for the worry and care we have visited
upon you.

AUTHOR UNKNOWN

FATHER

Hands that know
our suffering,
hands that feel
our pain,
hands that bear
our burdens,
hands that give
again,
hands that calm
and comfort,
hands that heal
and share,
hands that seek
compassion,
hands that love
and care,
hands of a father,
hands we know
in part,

hands that keep
revealing,
a kind and loving
heart.

THOMAS L. REID

Holidays

To My Father: A Toast

If faith is the assurance of things hoped for,
the conviction of things not seen,
I have the courage to believe today
because I have seen you
live,
dream,
work,
play,
and love—
without limit.

MARYANNE HANNAN

FOURTH OF JULY

On this day of independence, Lord of life and liberty, let freedom ring and let it begin with me, for it is easy in these shrill times to raise fists instead of flags of tolerance and peace. Remind us of our forebears' vision, sacrifice, and hunger for freedom that conceived today's star-spangled festivities. As parades pass in cadence of proud independence, may we recognize one another as brother and sister, all Your children. And in firecracker red glare, let us pledge anew to remain a land of the free and be wise, kind, and brave in the doing.

MARGARET ANNE HUFFMAN

Holidays

A FOURTH OF JULY TOAST

As we prepare to ooh and ah
Over the artwork in the sky,
Here's to fireworks,
Here's to summer,
And here's to America
On this festive Fourth of July!

BARBARA YOUNGER

LABOR DAY

O Lord, it's another Monday and we have to go to work!

This is part prayer, part lament, for we're tired, concerned, and sometimes bored. Does what we do matter? Is it worth the hustle and hassle to climb the ladder? We yearn to leave marks as visible as skyscrapers or bridges, to be connected with what we do, something that matters. Remind us that each one is called to special tasks, purposes, and jobs. Always there is that first call from You working through *our* work to help, heal, change a needful world.

O Lord, it's Monday: what possibilities do You have in mind?

MARGARET ANNE HUFFMAN

GRANDPARENT'S DAY

(the second Sunday of September)

They are inspiration, Lord of history, having the souls of playmates and wisdom of sages, these grandparents we honor on their special day. Gently wise, they know that like sunflowers ripening in today's autumn glory, children are best supported, not burdened; best encouraged, not reshaped, expecting them only to become all You intend. Bless and keep them, for the grandchildren are growing from their sturdy, life-giving roots.

MARGARET ANNE HUFFMAN

A Toast for Halloween

On this, the night of Hallows' Eve
We keep a festive mood;
We dress in colorful costumes
And sample sweetened food;
And as a jack-o'-lantern's face
Lights friends to our front door,
We toast those near
Or far from us,
And say a silent prayer to bless
Those dear, departed souls
Who have gone before.

SHEILA FORSYTH

It's Halloween

Moonlight disguises
Make midnight surprises
And pumpkins
Are not what they seem—
On Halloween!

Your best friends pull switches,
They're goblins and witches
And hoboes
And monsters of green—
On Halloween!

It's all a charade,
A scary masquerade.
Alone and afraid
You seem.
So scream!
It's Halloween!

Costumes surprise you
And masks hypnotize you

As ghosts dance around
And between—
On Halloween!

Black cats look suspicious
And bats get their wishes.
A hobo's conducting
The scene
On Halloween!

It's all a charade,
A scary masquerade.
Alone and afraid
You seem.
So scream!
It's Halloween!

REBECCA MCCLANAHAN

Holidays

A PRAYER OF THANKSGIVING

For leaves of yellow and scarlet,
For goldenrod's bright array,
For crisp November breezes,
And frisky squirrels at play;
For misted mornings and velvet nights,
For glowing harvest moon,
For crickets' tuneful chirping
On a sunny afternoon;
For families gathered together,
For marigolds in a bouquet,
For bounty from the earth to share
This blessed holiday,
We're thankful.

SHEILA FORSYTH

For Thanksgiving

(Soul Seeds)

The simplicity is overwhelming,
For what we plant, we also reap.

Lord, grant us soul seeds,
That we may plant them with love,
Water them with tears of compassion,
Nurture them with embraces of warmth,
Protect them from the storms of life.

Bless this bounty with grace and gentleness,
That the harvest will be abundant
In love, in trust, to be shared
With those closest to our hearts.

May we plant soul seeds for strength,
Harvested in hope this Thanksgiving,
For all the days and years that follow.

JUDITH A. LINDBERG

A Thanksgiving Prayer

We cannot thank you, God, enough
For all the gifts you give,
For life and breath, for joy and song
That fill each day we live.

With gratitude this special day
Our praise goes up to you
For loved ones whom we cherish,
For all they are and do.

Lord, thank you for companionship
With those who share this meal;
The ones not gathered here with us,
Let them Thy blessings feel.

And now, oh heavenly Spirit,
Descend on us, we pray;
Teach us to share the gifts we have
Today and every day.

Amen.

DORIS LAND MUELLER

Holidays

THANKSGIVING

We gather today, Lord of abundant life, as grateful children. Delighted and humbled by our bounty, we celebrate gifts of food and shelter, of colors that dance at dawn and dusk; we relish the scent of cooking foods, of burning leaves and summer's wet grass, of snowflake, of animal fur. We marvel at the intricacy of spiders' webs and fish bones, newborn babies and lines etched on faces of grandparents come for a visit today. All gifts from Your hand. When our meal is completed, leftovers stashed, and naps taken, we will leave replete, energized, and eager to go generously into the world and share our good fortune.

REV. LYNN JAMES

Each Chanukah Candle

As we light each Chanukah candle,
And watch our children's faces,
We pray for understanding
Among people of all races.

JILL WILLIAMS

Holidays

CELEBRATING FREEDOM
AT CHANUKAH

We gather together this Chanukah night
to recount the ancient story
of strength, hope, freedom, and light
as we remember the Maccabees who fought
with all their might
for what they believed to be right—
freedom for the Jewish people.

Our memory of the Maccabees reminds us
that a small group of people
can make a large difference in the world.
When we recall the miracle
of the oil lasting for eight days
we have faith that miracles are possible.

We join together to cherish our freedom
and freedom for all people.
We know that we must always fight for
the right to live what we believe.
We pray for strength, hope, freedom, and light—
the spirit of this Chanukah night.

SHERRI WAAS SHUNFENTHAL

Nes Gadol Haya Sham

Nes Gadol Haya Sham—
A great miracle happened there—
we say as we spin the dreidel,
the Hebrew letters swirling
into dizzy oneness
before they find themselves again.
These words hang over us, bless us,
as we take crisp, fragrant latkes
into our mouths,
as we peel gold foil back
from chocolate coins,
as we touch wick to waxy wick.
A great miracle happened there, yes,
but a great miracle is happening here, too:
just as one day's worth of oil
could burn for eight nights straight,
so can our one family's love
fill the entire room with light.

GAYLE BRANDEIS

THANK YOU FOR CHANUKAH

Laughter everywhere
Singing here and there
Dreidel spinning round and round
Watch it fall to the ground
Will I get some chocolate
Chanukah gelt?

Chanukah cards I love to read
Presents from family and friends
I overflow with feelings of thanks

Thank you for wonderful family
Thank you for wonderful friends
Thank you for delicious latkes
Thank you for great gifts
Thank you for eight
marvelous days to celebrate!

JENNIFER SHUNFENTHAL
AGE 9

Holidays

Chanukah

For these eight days
while the moon is dark:
within me, the light of my faith
outside me, the flame of each menorah candle
Both reaffirm my connection
to the One, creator of Light

ARLENE GAY LEVINE

CHRISTMAS EVE BLESSING

May the mystical peace
of this blessed Christmas Eve
remain in our hearts
throughout the New Year.

NOREEN BRAMAN

Holidays

AN IRISH CHRISTMAS TOAST

May peace and plenty be the first
To lift the latch on your door,
And happiness be guided
To your home
By the candle of Christmas.

AUTHOR UNKNOWN

THIS CHRISTMAS

May we set an extra place at the table this Christmas,
as we remember the hungry, the poor.

May we wrap an extra gift this Christmas, as we
remember the lonely, the confused.

May we give an extra hug this Christmas, as an
expression of love to those around us.

May we spend extra time in meditation this Christmas,
as we remember all the blessings we've received—
beautiful gifts of life and grace.

NORMA WOODBRIDGE

A Christmas Toast

Let's tip a glass to Christmas past
And times we held so dear,
For now's the time to reminisce
And sip a bit of cheer.
Dwell not on sorrow in our lives,
But raise our spirits high;
Though cherished ones may go their way,
Their memories never die.

Give prayer for virtues that we have,
Forget the ones we lack;
Keep our sights on future goals
And failure at our back.
Make a vow to treasured friends
To always keep in touch—
The ones we take for granted
Are the ones that mean so much.

Live our lives as best we can
That peers may one day say:
We left the world a better place
Because we passed this way.

C. DAVID HAY

Holidays

CHRISTMAS PRAYER

May the joy of the angels
That holy night
Resound in your heart
And bring you delight.

May the faith of the shepherds
Kneeling in prayer
Remind you of God's love
Everywhere.

May the wise men's devotion
That brought them so far
Be also, for you,
A guiding star.

THERESA MARY GRASS

CHRISTMAS BENEDICTION

May your barns be full of plenty,
And your heart be full of song.
May your house be full of laughter,
And friends, the whole year long.

May your days be full of wonder,
Merriment and peace,
With love and hope surrounding,
May Christmas joys increase.

NORMA WOODBRIDGE

Tiny Tim's Toast

(from *A Christmas Carol*)

Here's to us all!
God bless us every one!

CHARLES DICKENS
(1812–1870)

A KWANZAA COMMITMENT
(DECEMBER 26 - JANUARY 1)

Strive for discipline, dedication, and achievement in all you do. Dare struggle and sacrifice and gain the strength that comes from this. Build where you are and dare leave a legacy that will last as long as the sun shines and the water flows. Practice daily Umoja, Kujichagulia, Ujima, Ujamaa, Nia, Kuumba, and Imani. And may the wisdom of the ancestors always walk with us. May the year's end meet us laughing and stronger. May our children honor us by following our example in love and struggle. And at the end of next year, may we sit again together, in larger numbers, with greater achievement and closer to liberation and a higher level of human life.

HARAMBEE!   HARAMBEE!   HARAMBEE!
HARAMBEE!   HARAMBEE!   HARAMBEE!
HARAMBEE!

MAULANA KARENGA

(Dr. Maulana Karenga is the founder of Kwanzaa, a Pan-African holiday celebrated throughout the world African community. He is also professor and chair of the Department of Black Studies at California State University in Long Beach.)

Holidays

A New Year's Toast

May the joys be many
and the tears be few
Peace to the world
and much love to you

PATTY FORBES CHENG

PRAISE FOR THE NEW YEAR

Welcome in the New Year
As you would a friend;
One who brings twelve shining gifts
To last until year's end.
Harmony with others,
Faith in each new day;
All the kindness you can spare,
Goodwill in words you say.
Compassion for earth's creatures,
And hope for those in need;
Make peace with all of nature,
Make tolerance your creed.
Thoughtfulness and sharing,
Love spread far and near;
A thankfulness for living
To end a perfect year.

SHEILA FORSYTH

Holidays

THE NEW YEAR

A flower unblown; a book unread;
A tree with fruit unharvested;
A path untrod; a house whose rooms
Lack yet the heart's divine perfumes;
A landscape whose wide border lies
In silent shade, 'neath silent skies;
A treasure with its gifts concealed—
This is the year that for you waits
Beyond tomorrow's mystic gates.

HORATIO NELSON POWERS

FOURTEEN

SPECIAL

RETIREMENT

Every end is a beginning,
another mountain to climb
or space to pursue new possibilities, or withdraw
to the other side of the bank
under a great sprawling sycamore
where the river quietly flows
and just breathe

MARIAN OLSON

Special

A Bon Voyage Prayer

Dear God, who travels with us always, watch especially over _____ and _____ as they venture forth for fun. Guide their steps through foreign streets, and keep their eyes open, always open, to see the new and connect it to the known, to observe with alertness and curiosity. Help them to rest, to vacate the ordinary worries of ordinary days. Remind them to sit on benches, drink cool waters, and take long, breath-resting naps.

And when their feet weary and their minds are full, nudge them home to tell us stories. Amen.

MARTHA K. BAKER

Special

GRADUATION / NEW JOB / A MOVE

Give us courageous hearts and inquisitive minds, O God of beacons and stars, so that we will always be stretching and growing to fit the new world You call us into. Protect us during in-between times when we feel as vulnerable as a crab skittering across the sand to a new, larger shell. Guide our exploration; nudge us into waters of change. Always, always it is You inspiring the journey.

MARGARET ANNE HUFFMAN

Special

MOVING DAY

Roots are being ripped up, Lord of pilgrims
and explorers, as we say good-bye to friends,
neighborhood, familiarity. The moving van is
loaded, the maps marked with new routes. May
the memory of this place, these bonds, nourish
us in new places and times just as the embers of
a fire lay a foundation for the next. As we look
over our shoulders and in rearview mirrors of
what was, remind us that two things can be true
at once: new is scary, new is good. Hold our
hands, Lord, for we need a companion for the
journey between.

MARGARET ANNE HUFFMAN

Special

TOAST FOR AN
ACADEMIC REUNION

Today we toast our memories—
the students, athletes, and friends
we once were—reunited for a time,
reliving our shared past.
Everything that happened here
played its part in shaping us,
so we return to remember
the youth we were here.
We also honor those who
taught and encouraged us.
We remember old friends,
those with us now,
those who couldn't make it,
and those who are no longer with us.
Dear friends, lift your glasses with me
to our younger selves—their activities,
their plans, their promise.
May we always remember with gratitude
their part in making us who we are today.

Special

SUZANNE C. COLE

A TOOTH FAIRY TOAST

Here's to the old tooth under the pillow,
Here's to the space that it left behind,
Here's to the new tooth soon to follow,
Here's to the tooth fairy, generous and kind!

BARBARA YOUNGER

Special

Olde Scottish
Nighttime Blessing

(Note: This can be read as the last toast
of the evening before guests go to bed.)

May yer seatin be enthroned,
May yer castle be yer home;
May yer tub e'er overflow,
And yer love long embers glow.
May yer teethbrush be yer own,
And if ney, may it not be known;
May yer towel be always dry,
And yer spirits lifted high.
May yer mirror reflect yer heart,
And each day with a prayer do start;
May the Morning Son's first ray,
Be the light that guides yer way.
And when yer howse be still at night,
May e'er yer heart be right;
And the hurts ye hold, forgive,
That in peace yer soul may live.

JILL NOBLIT MACGREGOR

In Appreciation
of Single Parents

Great and wonderful, wondrous families who reflect You, O God, are far more than the sum of their missing parts. Our family portrait is missing nothing that truly matters, for we have love. Love overflowing *for* one another, abundant love *from* You, and love enough to *include* someone else if that should happen. Blessed by You, we're joyfully focusing on our bounty, not a missing number!

MARGARET ANNE HUFFMAN

Special

In Honor of a Stepfamily

Guide our *steps*, pathfinding God, as we move from *what was to what can be*. We want to become a family. Guide us to common ground. As we *step* closer, keep us from crowding one another; help us honor each one as unique, intriguing, special. And as we build new traditions, help us respect grief over losing old ones, for even in the midst of celebrating and rebuilding, there is mourning. *Step* closer, Lord, and guide us toward wholeness.

MARGARET ANNE HUFFMAN

Special

FAMILY VACATION

Even You, Lord of creation, rested. It's a sensible
plan we've overlooked, and our frantic comings
and going have frayed moods and dulled affections.
But now our suitcases are packed and we're leaving
on a family vacation. Ease the transition, for like
learning to skip or ride a bike, it's tricky to catch
on to the time-off rhythm. Set the pace, Lord of
all the time in the world, so we can savor this
interlude's quiet, subtle pleasures and one another.
A vacation is a marvelous place to collect thoughts
and restore our souls.

MARGARET ANNE HUFFMAN

Special

IN APPRECIATION
OF THE FAMILY PET

They love without strings attached, these loving beasts of Your hand, O God of amazing critters. Bless them, for they bless us even when they leave muddy paw prints on clean floors, ignore our commands, and shed on the furniture. Keep us worthy of their trust.

MARGARET ANNE HUFFMAN

Special

BLESSING OF THE ATHLETES

(Note: This poem can be customized for specific athletic events.
The italicized lines may be read in unison.)

Dear God,
As these athletes begin their journey/race, we
thank you for the opportunity to be together.

We are all grateful for health and the challenges of
this world.

We ask you to bless the hearts of these ath-
letes with health, patience, and good humor, as
they begin this great challenge. May they find in
themselves the strength and endurance that
reflects your glory.

We are all grateful for health and the challenges of
this world.

May every mile/part of this journey/race be
filled with your grace, we ask it in your name.
Amen.

DONNA W. GUTHRIE

Special

FIFTEEN

BENEDICTIONS

GO WITH THE
STRENGTH YOU HAVE

> Go with the strength you have.
> Go simply, lightly, gently,
> in search of Love.
> And the Spirit go with you.

KIAMU CAWIDRONE

IRISH BLESSING

May the blessing of light be on you,
light without and light within.
May the blessed sunlight shine upon you
and warm your heart
till it glows like a great fire
and strangers may warm themselves
as well as friends.

And may the light shine out of the eyes of you,
like a candle set in the window of a house,
bidding the wanderer to come in
out of the storm.

May the blessing of rain be on you;
the soft, sweet rain.
May it fall upon your spirit
so that little flowers may spring up
and shed their sweetness on the air.

And may the blessing of the great rains be on you,
to beat upon your spirit and wash it fair and clean;
and leave there many a shining pool
where the blue of heaven shines,
and sometimes a star.

May the blessing of the earth be on you,
the great, round earth;
may you ever have a kindly greeting for people
as you're going along the roads.

And now may the Lord bless you,
and bless you kindly. Amen.

AUTHOR UNKNOWN

MAY THE LONG TIME SUN SHINE UPON YOU

May the long time sun shine upon you
all love surround you, and the pure light
within you guide you all the way on.

AUTHOR UNKNOWN

Benedictions

AUTHOR INDEX

Author Index

PERMISSIONS AND ACKNOWLEDGMENTS

Grateful acknowledgment is made to the authors and publishers for the use of the following material. Every effort has been made to contact original sources. If notified, the publishers will be pleased to rectify an omission in future editions.

Atheneum Books for Young Readers, an imprint of Simon & Schuster Children's Publishing Division from *I Am Wings* by Ralph Fletcher. Text copyright © 1994 by Ralph Fletcher.

Martha K. Baker for "A Bon Voyage Prayer."

Bantam Doubleday Dell Publishing Group for "A Birthday Wish" by Dorothy Nell McDonald from *Poems That Touch the Heart*, compiled by A. L. Alexander. Copyright © 1941 by Bantam Doubleday Dell; "If" by Rudyard Kipling from *Rudyard Kipling's Verse Definitive Edition* by Rudyard Kipling, © 1940 by Elsie Kipling Bambridge, Doubleday and Company Inc.

Judy A. Barnes for "Overheard at a Cowboy's Wedding."

James Bertolino for "The Forty Poem" and "A Wedding Toast."

Noreen Braman for "Christmas Eve Blessing."

Gayle Brandeis for "Nes Gadol Haya Sham."

Danielle Brigante for "A Blessing for Family."

Jayne England Byrne for "This Gathering of Generations."

Elizabeth Campbell for "From This Day Forth."

Patty Forbes Cheng for "A New Year's Toast."

SuzAnne C. Cole for "A Mother's Day Toast" and "Toast for an Academic Reunion."

Kathy Conde for "What Makes You Aware."

Deborah Cooper for "Memorial Prayer," "Morning Prayer," "Prayer of Blessings," and "Winter Comes."

Darlene A. Croce for "A Toast for Your New Home."

The Crown Publishing Group for "Bless Our Meal" by Mount St. Mary's Abbey from *One Hundred Graces* by Maria Kelly and Jack Kelly. Copyright © 1992 by Maria Kelly and Jack Kelly. Published by Bell Tower, an imprint of Harmony Books, a division of Crown Publishers Inc.

Mary Maude Daniels for "Gratitude."

Annie Dougherty for "Speaking to Angels."

Alice Faye Duncan for "Roots."

Jan Dunlap for "Wedding Toast: A Marriage for All Seasons."

Mary Eastham for "For Our Anniversary."

Lori Eberhardy for "A Celebration" and "The Starmaker."

Kim V. Engelmann for "A Christening Prayer."

Susan J. Erickson for "Housewarming Toast," "Toast to the Now," and "Valentine's Day Toast."

Ida Fasel for "Golden Wedding Anniversary."

Maureen Tolman Flannery for "As You Set Off."

Sheila Forsyth for "Praise for the New Year," "A Prayer of Thanksgiving," and "A Toast for Halloween."

Melissa J. Graham for "House Blessing."

Theresa Mary Grass for "Christmas Prayer."

Donna W. Guthrie for "Blessing of the Athletes."

Maryanne Hannan for "To My Father: A Toast."

C. David Hay for "A Christmas Toast."

Margaret Anne Huffman for "Easter," "Family Vacation," "Fourth of July," "Graduation/New Job/A Move," "Grandparent's Day," "In Appreciation of Single Parents," "In Appreciation of the Family Pet," "In Celebration of the Family," "In Honor of a Stepfamily," "Labor Day," "Milestone Anniversary," "Moving Day," and "Second Marriage."

The Iona Community for "Go with the Strength You Have" from *In Spirit and In Truth* by Kiamu Cawidrome. Copyright © 1991 by Iona Community, Scotland. Used by permission of the Iona Community.

Rev. Lynn James for "Earth Day" and "Thanksgiving."

Paula E. Kirman for "On Passover, We Remember."

Alfred A. Knopf Inc. for "St. Patrick's Day" from *Toasts: Over 1,500 of the Best Toasts, Sentiments, Blessings* by Paul Dickson. Copyright © 1991 by Paul Dickson. Reprinted by permission of Crown Publishers Inc.

Alfred A. Knopf Inc. for "Remembrance" and "You Were Born Together" from *The Prophet* by Kahlil Gibran. Copyright © 1923 and renewed 1951 by Administrators CTA of Kahlil Gibran Estate and Mary G. Gibran; "Each Day" and "Thanks" from *Markings* by Dag Hammarskjöld, trans., Sjoberg/Auden. Translation copyright © 1964 by Alfred A. Knopf Inc. and Faber & Faber Ltd. Reprinted by permission of Alfred A. Knopf Inc.

Stephen Kopel for "A Grace for Friends."

Norbert Krapf for "The Riddle of Three Words."

Arlene Gay Levine for "Always," "Chanukah," and "Going for the Gold."

Judith A. Lindberg for "For Thanksgiving" (originally titled "Soul Seeds").

Janet Lombard for "A Shared Bond."

Patrick E. Loukes for "Grace of Compassion."

Jill Noblit MacGregor for "Olde Scottish Nighttime Blessing."

Amy Mallett for "A Wish for the Graduate."

Betti J. Marvel for "From Mom, On Graduation Day."

Rebecca McClanahan for "It's Halloween."

Maude Meehan for "To the Four Winds."

Dawn M. Mueller for "Home Sweet Home."

Doris Land Mueller for "If (for Mothers)" and "A Thanksgiving Prayer."

Tim Myers for "For a New House."

Allison J. Nichol for "They Know."

Susan Norton for "Destiny" and "Mother, You Inspire Me."

Marian Olson for "A Housewarming Toast," "Retirement," and "Sisters."

Nita Penfold for "Advice to My Niece at Her Birth."

Penguin Putnam Inc. for "In One Another's Souls" from *Wedding Readings* by Eleanor Munro. Copyright © 1989. Adapted by Eleanor Munro from A. J. Arberry translation of Jalal-Al-Din Rumi. Used by permission of Viking Penguin, a division of Penguin Putnam Inc.

Sharon Ostrander Reed for "A Daughter's Wedding Day Tribute."

Thomas L. Reid for "Father."

Linda Robertson for "Baby Fair."

Marion Schoeberlein for "The Finest Tribute."

Gaar Scott for "Wedding Toast."

Self-Counsel Press for "Each Chanukah Candle" by Jill Williams from *Quick Notes and Fast Quotes for Every Occasion*. Copyright © 1991, 1992 by International Self-Counsel Press Ltd. Used with permission of the author and Self-Counsel Press.

Rabbi Rami M. Shapiro for "Liberation" and "A Parent's Prayer."

Jennifer Shunfenthal for "Thank You for Chanukah."

Sherri Waas Shunfenthal for "Celebrating Freedom at Chanukah" and "Two Hearts."

Simon & Schuster for "For There Is No Friend Like a Sister" by Christina Rossetti from *Selected Poems of Christina Rossetti*, edited by Marya Zaturenska (New York: Macmillan. Copyright © 1970). Reprinted with permission of Simon & Schuster.

Kate Simpson for "New Baby."

Jean Conder Soule for "A Child's Noontime Grace."

Jennifer M. Spencer for "Hope" and "Soul Mates."

Anne Spring for "Family Re-Union," "Memorial Service," and "Prayer for a New Baby."

Molly Srode for "Baby Blessing."

Joan Stephen for "The Blooming of Easter," "In Memoriam," "Philosophy," and "Toast to Daughters."

Paula Timpson for "Christening."

The University of Sankore Press for "A Kwanzaa Commitment" (originally titled "Tamshi La Tutaonana") from *Kwanzaa: A Celebration of Family, Community and Culture* by Maulana Karenga. Copyright © 1998. Used with permission of The University of Sankore Press.

Anne Vogel for "A Grace for a Gathering."

Nancy Lynch Weiss for "A House Blessing."

Norma Woodbridge for "Christmas Benediction" and "This Christmas."

Barbara Younger for "A Child's Birthday Grace," "A Christening Celebration Grace," "A Fourth of July Toast," "A Memorial for a Pet," and "A Tooth Fairy Toast."

Permissions compiled by Cheryl Edmonson